Alexander Graham Bell

Barbara Kramer

NATIONAL
GEOGRAPHIC

Washington, D.C.

For Callie —B.K.

The publisher and author gratefully acknowledge the expert review
of this book by Alexander Graham Bell National Historic Site of Canada.

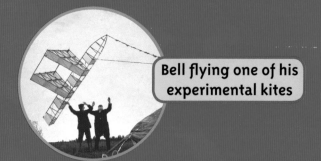

Bell flying one of his
experimental kites

Paperback ISBN: 978-1-4263-1935-8
Reinforced Library Binding ISBN: 978-1-4263-1936-5

Book design by YAY! Design

Photo credits

Cover, Harris And Ewing/National Geographic Creative; cover (background), Mansell/Mansell/Time & Life Pictures/Getty Images; top border
of page (throughout), Seamartini Graphics/Shutterstock; vocabulary box art, Svetlana Prikhnenko/Shutterstock; 1, The Print Collector/Print
Collector/Getty Images; 2, Bell Collection/National Geographic Creative; 4, Bell Collection/National Geographic Creative; 5, Stock Montage/
Stock Montage/Getty Images; 6, Bell Collection/National Geographic Creative; 7, Bell Collection/National Geographic Creative; 8, Bell Family/
National Geographic Creative; 9, Dr. Gilbert H. Grosvenor/National Geographic Creative; 10 (UP), Hulton Archive/Getty Images; 10 (LO), Liszt
Collection/Heritage Images/Getty Images; 11 (UP), Oxford Science Archive/Print Collector/Getty Images; 11 (LO), Doug Pearson/JAI/Corbis; 13,
Bell Collection/National Geographic Creative; 14, SSPL/Getty Images; 15, Bell Homestead National Historic Site, Brantford, Ontario, Canada; 16,
Bell Collection/National Geographic Creative; 17, Bell Family/National Geographic Creative; 18, Ryan McVay/Photodisc/Getty Images; 19, The
Granger Collection, NYC—All rights reserved; 20 (UP), picturelibrary/Alamy; 20 (LO), Underwood & Underwood/Corbis; 21, Bettmann/Corbis;
22, The Granger Collection, NYC—All rights reserved; 23, The Granger Collection, NYC—All rights reserved; 24-25 (Background), ZanyZeus/
Shutterstock; 24 (CTR), Bell Collection/National Geographic Creative; 24 (CTR), Dr. Gilbert H. Grosvenor/National Geographic Creative; 24 (LO),
Universal History Archive/Getty Images; 25 (UP), Gilbert H. Grosvenor Collection of Photographs of the Alexander Graham Bell Family/Library
of Congress; 25 (CTR LE), Anastasija Popova/Shutterstock; 25 (CTR RT), Time Life Pictures/Mansell/The LIFE Picture Collection/Getty Images; 25
(LO), Bell Collection/National Geographic Creative; 26 (UP), Visions of America/UIG via/Getty Images; 26 (LO), Gilbert H. Grosvenor Collection
of Photographs of the Alexander Graham Bell Family/Library of Congress; 26-27, dencg/Shutterstock; 27, National Geographic/National Geo-
graphic Creative; 28, Bell Collection/National Geographic Creative; 28-29, dencg/Shutterstock; 30 (UP), Doug Pearson/JAI/Corbis; 30 (CTR),
Dr. Gilbert H. Grosvenor/National Geographic Creative; 30, Bell Collection/National Geographic Creative; 31 (UP), The Granger Collection,
NYC—All rights reserved; 31 (CTR RT), iconeer/iStockphoto; 31 (CTR LE), Buyenlarge/Getty Images; 31 (LO), Miljan Mladenovic/Shutterstock; 32
(UPLE), Bell Collection/National Geographic/Getty Images; 32 (UPRT), Monkey Business Images/Shutterstock; 32 (CTR LE), Universal History Archive/
Getty Images; 32 (CTR RT), huyangshu/Shutterstock; 32 (LOLE), Bell Collection/National Geographic Creative; 32 (LORT), pirita/Shutterstock

National Geographic supports K–12 educators with ELA Common Core Resources.
Visit natgeoed.org/commoncore for more information.

Table of Contents

An Inventor and Teacher

Can you imagine a world with no telephones? You would not be able to call your friends or text them with exciting news. If you needed a ride home, you could not call anyone to let them know. Thanks to Alexander Graham Bell, we now have telephones to make our lives easier.

In His Own Words

"The inventor looks upon the world and is not contented with things as they are. He wants to improve whatever he sees."

A Boy in Scotland

Bell was born on March 3, 1847, in Edinburgh (EH-den-ber-ruh), Scotland. He was the second of three sons. His grandfather and father were also named Alexander Bell. So he went by the nickname Aleck.

That's a Fact! Bell did not have a middle name. He added the name Graham when he was 11 years old. His parents were not upset. They liked his new name.

Bell at age 15

Bell's grandfather and father were both speech teachers. They helped people learn to speak more clearly.

Bell's mother, Eliza, was almost totally deaf. She used an ear tube to help her hear.

Words to Know

EAR TUBE: A horn-shaped tool that guides sound to the ear

A young Bell (right) with his father and grandfather

Exploring

As a boy, Bell enjoyed music. He could listen to a song, then sit down and play it on the piano. He could remember the notes he heard. Then he played them back.

He liked science, too. He collected shells, birds' eggs, butterflies, and bugs. Later he added skeletons of small animals, such as frogs and mice.

Bell continued to play music all his life.

Royal High School

His mother homeschooled him until he was 10. When he was 11, he went to Royal High School. He graduated when he was 14 years old.

That's a Fact!

Bell created his first invention when he was 11 years old. It was a machine to remove the husk, or outer covering, from grains of wheat.

Young Teacher

In 1863, Bell began teaching speech and music. He was 16 years old. Some of his students were older than he was!

He also studied his father's Visible Speech system. The system used symbols (SIM-bulls) to show how the mouth, tongue, and lips make sounds. Bell helped his father demonstrate (DEM-un-strate) how it worked to groups of people.

Words to Know

VISIBLE: Able to be seen

SYMBOL: A letter or picture used instead of words

DEMONSTRATE: To show how something works

[ENGLISH ALPHABET OF VISIBLE SPEECH,
Expressed in the Names of Numbers and Objects.]

[Pronounce the Nos.] — [Names.] — [Name the Objects.]

1.
2.
3.
4.
5.
6.
7.
8.

[EXERCISE.]

One by one.
Two or three.
Four at once.
Five o'clock.
Half-past six.
Seven-thirty.
Eight to nine.
Ten or twelve.
Twice two, four.
Twice three, six.
Four and four, eight.
Nine and two, eleven.
Twice or thrice.

Two, a couple.
Twelve, a dozen.
Twenty, a score.
A book-case.
A few books.
New book-shelves.
A silver watch.
A gold watch.
The watch-key.
A good saw.
Cap and feather.
Tongs and shovel.
Sugar-tongs.

A hunting whip.
A table lamp.
A bunch of onions.
Corns and bunions.
A ship's boat.
A sailing boat.
Cart and horse.
A round tent.
Rows of houses.
A dog-kennel.
A little monkey.
A pretty cage.
A green canary.

This chart shows symbols in the Visible Speech system.

Bell and his father later believed the Visible Speech system could help deaf people learn to talk.

A New Country

The Bell family moved to London in 1865. Bell studied and taught there. At one school, he used his father's Visible Speech system to teach deaf children.

Sadly, Bell's younger brother died from a lung disease (di-ZEEZ) in 1867. Three years later, his older brother died from the same disease.

London in the mid-1800s

The Bell family's home in Ontario

Bell's parents said it was because of the polluted (puh-LOO-ted) air in the large city.

In 1870, Bell and his parents sailed to Canada. They moved into a home in Ontario (on-TARE-ee-oh). Bell's father said he liked the fresh, clean air there.

Words to Know

DISEASE: An illness
POLLUTED: Dirty, not safe

15

Bell (top row right) with students at the Boston school where he taught

Bell's father traveled to Boston, Massachusetts. He met the principal of a school for deaf people. The school was looking for a teacher. Bell's father said his son would be good for the job. In 1871, Bell began teaching there.

In Boston, there were many inventors. Bell had ideas for inventions, too. He taught during the day. Then he worked on his inventions late into the night. It did not give him much time for sleep.

A page from Bell's notebook where he made sketches of his inventions

A Big Idea

At that time, the telegraph was the fastest

Telegraph

way to send messages. Bell wanted to make it work faster. He needed to find a way to send more than one message over a wire at a time.

While he was working on that, he got an even bigger idea. What if voices could travel by wire from place to place? That would be much faster than the telegraph.

Bell was not good at building things. He needed someone who could turn his sketches, or drawings, into a working machine. In January 1875, Thomas Watson became his assistant (uh–SIS–tant).

Bell (left) in his laboratory with his assistant, Watson (right)

Bell and Watson tried one thing, then another. Many of their experiments did not work. But they did not give up.

Telephone transmitter

Telephone receiver

More than a year later, on March 10, 1876, Bell was ready for another test. "Mr. Watson—come here— I want to see you," he shouted into his machine. Watson was working in another room. He ran to Bell with exciting news. He had heard Bell's voice through the wire! That was the very first telephone call.

Bell and Watson working together in Boston in 1877

Presenting the Telephone

In June 1876, Bell demonstrated his telephone at a large fair in Philadelphia (fill-uh-DEL-fee-uh), Pennsylvania. People were amazed.

Bell speaking into his telephone in front of a large crowd

The Bell Telephone Company

They lined up to take turns listening and speaking on the telephone.

A year later, Bell and three other men created the Bell Telephone Company. They charged people a fee to use telephones in their homes and places of work.

7 Cool Facts About Bell

1

Fifteen-year-old Bell and his older brother used rubber, tin, and wood to make a talking skull.

2

Bell married Mabel Hubbard. She had been one of his students. Mabel had lost her hearing because of a childhood illness.

3

Bell had a picture of an owl hanging in his lab. His wife gave it to him as a joke because he worked so late at night.

4

Bell was very interested in flight. He built giant kites to help him learn more about it.

5

Bell trained his horse well. When Bell clapped once, the horse took Bell to his lab. Two claps meant "go home."

6

On January 25, 1915, Bell made the first coast-to-coast telephone call from New York to California.

7

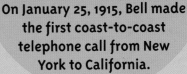

Bell encouraged his ten grandchildren to explore new ideas. He created more than 100 experiments for the children to do.

New Adventures

The Bell family's second home in Cape Breton in Canada

Bell and his family moved to Washington, D.C., in 1879. Bell set up a lab and began working on different inventions.

1847
Born in Edinburgh, Scotland, on March 3

1858
Creates his first invention

1862
Builds a talking machine with his older brother

In 1898, Bell became president of the National Geographic Society. He made *National Geographic* magazine better by adding photographs and maps from places all around the world.

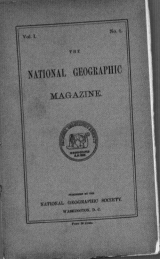

1863
Begins teaching speech and music

1870
Moves to Ontario, Canada

1871
Begins teaching at a school for the deaf in Boston, Massachusetts

Helping Others

Bell works with Helen Keller (left), a woman who overcame being both deaf and unable to speak.

1876

Makes the first telephone call to his assistant on March 10

1877

Marries Mabel Hubbard on July 11

Bell died on August 2, 1922. In his honor, the whole telephone system was shut down for one minute.

Bell never stopped experimenting. He spent his life helping others in many ways. He taught deaf people to talk. His telephone changed the way we communicate. It made our lives easier, and it made Bell one of the best known inventors in the world.

1879
Moves to Washington, D.C.

1915
Makes the first coast-to-coast telephone call

1922
Dies on August 2

Be a Quiz Whiz!

See how many questions you can get right! Answers are at the bottom of page 31.

Bell was born in _____.
A. Ontario
B. Edinburgh
C. Boston
D. London

Bell's first invention was _____.
A. A telegraph
B. A talking machine
C. A telephone
D. A machine to remove husks from grains of wheat

Bell began teaching speech and music when he was _____ years old.
A. 16
B. 18
C. 21
D. 25

4

Before Bell invented the telephone, the fastest way to send messages was by _____.
A. Email
B. Steamboat
C. Telegraph
D. Train

Bell made the first coast-to-coast telephone call in _____.
A. 1876
B. 1915
C. 1920
D. 1922

5

6

In 1876, Bell showed his telephone at a large fair in _____.
A. Boston
B. New York
C. Washington, D.C.
D. Philadelphia

The first president to have a telephone in the White House was _____.
A. Lincoln
B. Garfield
C. Hayes
D. Jackson

7

DEMONSTRATE: To show how something works

DISEASE: An illness

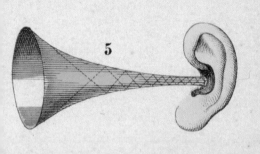

EAR TUBE: A horn-shaped tool that guides sound to the ear

POLLUTED: Dirty, not safe

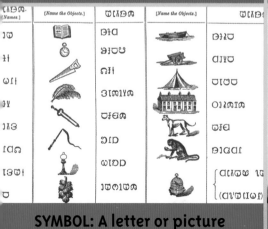

SYMBOL: A letter or picture used instead of words

VISIBLE: Able to be seen